T0204997

THE NIGHT BEFORE CHRISTMAS
AND OTHER POEMS

THE NIGHT BEFORE CHRISTMAS
AND OTHER POEMS

SIRIUS

Picture Credits

Mary Evans Picture Library: p8, p9, p11, p12, p13, p15, p17, p18, p19, p21, p22, p23, p24, p25, pp26, p27, p29, p31, p32, p33, p34, p35.

SIRIUS

This edition published in 2024 by Sirius Publishing, a division of Arcturus Publishing Limited,
26/27 Bickels Yard, 151–153 Bermondsey Street,
London SE1 3HA

ISBN: 978-1-3988-4313-4
AD011527NT

Printed in China

Contents

Introduction

Originally published in 1823, Clement Clarke Moore's "A Visit from St. Nicholas" has endured as a Christmas favorite for over two centuries. Filled with adventure and rip-roaring rhythm, Moore's depiction of Christmas and St. Nicholas has greatly contributed to the public's perception of Santa Claus and Christmas Eve. Published here is the 1931 edition of "The Night Before Christmas" accompanied by Arthur Rackham's incredible illustrations.

This festive collection of poems also includes works by a range of poets who highlight the warmth, wonder, and magic of Christmas and the colder months. John Clare's "Christmas Time" lays out the traditions of the season and George Wither's "Our Joyful Feast" exudes a lively charm. Also included are works by William Wordsworth, Henry Wadsworth Longfellow, Alexander Pushkin, and many more. So, settle down and immerse yourself in these merry verses about the hours spent among frosty trees, delicious feasts, and the flickering glow of a burning Yule log.

THE · NIGHT
BEFORE · CHRISTMAS

BY
CLEMENT · C · MOORE · LL·D·

ILLUSTRATED · BY
ARTHUR · RACKHAM

'Twas the night before Christmas, when all through the house
Not a creature was stirring, not even a mouse;
The stockings were hung by the chimney with care
In hopes that St. Nicholas soon would be there;

The children were nestled all snug in their
beds,
While visions of sugar-plums danced in their
heads;
And Mamma in her kerchief, and I in my cap,
Had just settled our brains for a long winter's
nap,

The children were nestled all snug in their beds

When out on the lawn there arose such a clatter,
I sprang from the bed to see what was the matter.
Away to the window I flew like a flash,
Tore open the shutters and threw up the sash.

The moon on the breast of the new-fallen
snow
Gave the lustre of midday to objects below,
When, what to my wondering eyes should
appear,
But a miniature sleigh, and eight tiny reindeer,

With a little old driver, so lively and
quick,

I knew in a moment it must be St. Nick.

More rapid than eagles his coursers they came,

And he whistled, and shouted, and called them
by name:

"Now, *Dasher!* now, *Dancer!* now, *Prancer*
and *Vixen!*
On, *Comet!* on, *Cupid!* on, *Donner* and *Blitzen!*
To the top of the porch! to the top of the wall!
Now dash away! dash away! dash away all!"

As dry leaves that before the wild hurricane
fly,
When they meet with an obstacle, mount to the
sky;
So up to the house-top the coursers they flew,
With the sleigh full of Toys, and St. Nicholas too.

And then, in a twinkling, I heard on the roof
The prancing and pawing of each little hoof.
As I drew in my head, and was turning around,
Down the chimney St. Nicholas came with a bound.

He was dressed all in fur, from his head to
his foot,
And his clothes were all tarnished with ashes
and soot;
A bundle of Toys he had flung on his back,
And he looked like a pedlar just opening his
pack.

His eyes—how they twinkled! his dimples how merry!
His cheeks were like roses, his nose like a cherry!
His droll little mouth was drawn up like a bow,
And the beard of his chin was as white as the snow;

Filled all the stockings

The stump of a pipe he held tight in his teeth,
And the smoke it encircled his head like a wreath;
He had a broad face and a little round belly,
That shook when he laughed, like a bowlful of jelly.

He was chubby and plump, a right jolly old elf,

And I laughed when I saw him, in spite of
  myself;

A wink of his eye and a twist of his head

Soon gave me to know I had nothing to dread.

He spoke not a word, but went straight to
his work,
And filled all the stockings; then turned with a
  jerk,
And laying his finger aside of his nose,
And giving a nod, up the chimney he rose;

He sprang to his sleigh, to his team gave a whistle,

And away they all flew like the down of a thistle.

But I heard him exclaim, ere he drove out of sight,

HAPPY CHRISTMAS

TO

ALL

AND

TO ALL

A GOOD NIGHT

CHRISTMAS
POEMS

Ceremonies for Christmas

ROBERT HERRICK

Come, bring with a noise,
  My merry, merry boys,
The Christmas Log to the firing;
  While my good Dame, she
  Bids ye all be free;
And drink to your heart's desiring.

With the last year's brand
  Light the new block, and
For good success in his spending,
  On your Psaltries play,
  That sweet luck may
Come while the log is a-tending;

Drink now the strong beer,
   Cut the white loaf here,
The while the meat is a-shredding;
   For the rare mince-pie
   And the plums stand by
To fill the paste that's a-kneading.

Give Me Holly

CHRISTINA ROSSETTI

But give me holly, bold and jolly,
Honest, prickly, shining holly;
Pluck me holly leaf and berry
For the day when I make merry

The Snow-Storm

RALPH WALDO EMERSON

Announced by all the trumpets of the sky,
Arrives the snow, and, driving o'er the fields,
Seems nowhere to alight; the whited air
Hides hills and woods, the river, and the heaven,
And veils the farm-house at the garden's end.
The sled and traveler stopped, the courier's feet
Delayed, all friends shut out, the housemates sit
Around the radiant fireplace, enclosed
In a tumultuous privacy of storm.

Come see the north wind's masonry.
Out of an unseen quarry evermore
Furnished with tile, the fierce artificer
Curves his white bastions with projected roof
Round every windward stake, or tree, or door.
Speeding, the myriad-handed, his wild work
So fanciful, so savage, nought cares he
For number or proportion. Mockingly,

On coop or kennel he hangs Parian wreaths;
A swan-like form invests the hidden thorn;
Fills up the farmer's lane from wall to wall,
Maugre the farmer's sighs; and, at the gate,
A tapering turret overtops the work.
And when his hours are numbered, and the
    world
Is all his own, retiring, as he were not,
Leaves, when the sun appears, astonished Art
To mimic in slow structures, stone by stone,
Built in an age, the mad wind's night-work,
The frolic architecture of the snow.

The Hanging of the Holly

CLINTON SCOLLARD

The holly is for happiness;
    Hang it, hang it high,
When the holy morn we bless
    Shows its rose along the sky!

The holly is for heartsome cheer;
    Hang it, hang it high,
While the glory of the year
    Lights the heights of all the sky!

The holly is for home-side mirth;
    Hang it, hang it high,
Till the dearest day of earth
    Fades in shades along the sky!

The Oxen

THOMAS HARDY

Christmas Eve, and twelve of the clock.
"Now they are all on their knees,"
An elder said as we sat in a flock
By the embers in fireside ease.

We pictured the meek mild creatures, where
They dwelt in their strawy pen,
Nor did it occur to one of us there
To doubt they were kneeling then.

So fair a fancy few would weave
In these years! Yet, I feel
If someone said on Christmas Eve,
"Come; see the oxen kneel,

"In the lonely barton by yonder coomb,
Our childhood used to know,"
I should go with him in the gloom,
Hoping it might be so.

The Darkling Thrush

THOMAS HARDY

I leant upon a coppice gate
  When Frost was spectre-gray,
And Winter's dregs made desolate
  The weakening eye of day.
The tangled bine-stems scored the sky
  Like strings of broken lyres,
And all mankind that haunted nigh
  Had sought their household fires.

The land's sharp features seemed to be
  The Century's corpse outleant,
His crypt the cloudy canopy,
  The wind his death-lament.
The ancient pulse of germ and birth
  Was shrunken hard and dry,
And every spirit upon earth
  Seemed fervourless as I.

At once a voice arose among
　　The bleak twigs overhead
In a full-hearted evensong
　　Of joy illimited;
An aged thrush, frail, gaunt, and small,
　　In blast-beruffled plume,
Had chosen thus to fling his soul
　　Upon the growing gloom.

So little cause for carollings
　　Of such ecstatic sound
Was written on terrestrial things
　　Afar or nigh around,
That I could think there trembled through
　　His happy good-night air
Some blessed Hope, whereof he knew
　　And I was unaware.

Minstrels

WILLIAM WORDSWORTH

The minstrels played their Christmas tune
To-night beneath my cottage-eaves;
While, smitten by a lofty moon,
The encircling laurels, thick with leaves,
Gave back a rich and dazzling sheen,
That overpowered their natural green.

Through hill and valley every breeze
Had sunk to rest with folded wings:
Keen was the air, but could not freeze,
Nor check, the music of the strings;
So stout and hardy were the band
That scraped the chords with strenuous hand.

And who but listened?—till was paid
Respect to every inmate's claim,
The greeting given, the music played
In honour of each household name,
Duly pronounced with lusty call,
And "Merry Christmas" wished to all.

Winter Morning

ALEXANDER PUSHKIN

Frost and sun—the day is wondrous!
Thou still art slumbering, charming friend.
'Tis time, O Beauty, to awaken:
Ope thine eyes, now in sweetness closed,
To meet the Northern Dawn of Morning
Thyself a north-star do thou appear!

Last night, remember, the storm scolded,
And darkness floated in the clouded sky;
Like a yellow, clouded spot
Thro' the clouds the moon was gleaming,—
And melancholy thou wert sitting—
But now ... thro' the window cast a look:

Stretched beneath the heavens blue
Carpet-like magnificent,
In the sun the snow is sparkling;
Dark alone is the wood transparent,

And thro' the hoar gleams green the fir,
And under the ice the rivulet sparkles.

Entire is lighted with diamond splendor
Thy chamber ... with merry crackle
The wood is crackling in the oven.
To meditation invites the sofa.
But know you? In the sleigh not order why
The brownish mare to harness?

Over the morning snow we gliding
Trust we shall, my friend, ourselves
To the speed of impatient steed;
Visit we shall the fields forsaken,
The woods, dense but recently,
And the banks so dear to me.

Christmas Time

JOHN CLARE

Glad Christmas comes, and every hearth
   Makes room to give him welcome now,
E'en want will dry its tears in mirth,
   And crown him with a holly bough;
Though tramping 'neath a winter sky,
   O'er snowy paths and rimy stiles,
The housewife sets her spinning by
   To bid him welcome with her smiles.
Each house is swept the day before,
   And windows stuck with evergreens,
The snow is besom'd from the door,
   And comfort the crowns the cottage scenes.
Gilt holly, with its thorny pricks,
   And yew and box, with berries small,
These deck the unused candlesticks,
   And pictures hanging by the wall.
Neighbours resume their annual cheer,
   Wishing, with smiles and spirits high,

Glad Christmas and a happy year
    To every morning passer-by;
Milkmaids their Christmas journeys go,
    Accompanied with favour'd swain;
And children pace the crumpling snow,
    To taste their granny's cake again.

The shepherd, now no more afraid,
    Since custom doth the chance bestow,
Starts up to kiss the giggling maid
    Beneath the branch of mistletoe
That 'neath each cottage beam is seen,
    With pearl-like berries shining gay;
The shadow still of what hath been,
    Which fashion yearly fades away.

The singing waits—a merry throng,
    At early morn, with simple skill,
Yet imitate the angel's song
    And chaunt their Christmas ditty still;
And, 'mid the storm that dies and swells
    By fits, in hummings softly steals

The music of the village bells,
    Ringing around their merry peals.

When this is past, a merry crew,
    Bedecked in masks and ribbons gay,
The Morris Dance, their sports renew,
    And act their winter evening play.
The clown turned king, for penny praise,
    Storms with the actor's strut and swell,
And harlequin, a laugh to raise,
    Wears his hunch-back and tinkling bell.

And oft for pence and spicy ale,
    With winter nosegays pinned before,
The wassail-singer tells her tale,
    And drawls her Christmas carols o'er.
While 'prentice boy, with ruddy face,
    And rime-bepowdered dancing locks,
From door to door, with happy face,
    Runs round to claim his "Christmas-box."

The block upon the fire is put,
    To sanction custom's old desires,
And many a fagot's bands are cut
    For the old farmer's Christmas fires;
Where loud-tongued gladness joins the throng,
    And Winter meets the warmth of May,
Till, feeling soon the heat too strong,
    He rubs his shins and draws away.

While snows the window-panes bedim,
    The fire curls up a sunny charm,
Where, creaming o'er the pitcher's rim,
    The flowering ale is set to warm.
Mirth full of joy as summer bees
    Sits there its pleasures to impart,
And children, 'tween their parents' knees,
    Sing scraps of carols off by heart.

And some, to view the winter weathers,
    Climb up the window seat with glee,
Likening the snow to falling feathers,
    In fancy's infant ecstasy;

Laughing, with superstitious love,
　　O'er visions wild that youth supplies,
Of people pulling geese above,
　　And keeping Christmas in the skies.

As though the homestead trees were drest,
　　In lieu of snow, with dancing leaves,
As though the sun-dried martin's nest,
　　Instead of ic'cles hung the eves;
The children hail the happy day—
　　As if the snow were April's grass,
And pleased, as 'neath the warmth of May,
　　Sport o'er the water froze to glass.

Thou day of happy sound and mirth,
　　That long with childish memory stays,
How blest around the cottage hearth,
　　I met thee in my younger days,
Harping, with rapture's dreaming joys,
　　On presents which thy coming found,
The welcome sight of little toys,

The Christmas gift of cousins round.
About the glowing hearth at night,
   The harmless laugh and winter tale
Go round; while parting friends delight
   To toast each other o'er their ale.
The cotter oft with quiet zeal
   Will, musing, o'er his bible lean;
While, in the dark the lovers steal,
   To kiss and toy behind the screen.

Old customs! Oh! I love the sound,
   However simple they may be;
Whate'er with time hath sanction found,
   Is welcome, and is dear to me,
Pride grows above simplicity,
   And spurns them from her haughty mind;
And soon the poet's song will be
   The only refuge they can find.

Old Santeclaus

ANONYMOUS

Old SANTECLAUS with much delight
His reindeer drives this frosty night,
O'er chimney-tops, and tracks of snow,
To bring his yearly gifts to you.

The steady friend of virtuous youth,
The friend of duty, and of truth,
Each Christmas eve he joys to come
Where love and peace have made their home.

Through many houses he has been,
And various beds and stockings seen;
Some, white as snow, and neatly mended,
Others, that seemed for pigs intended.

Where e'er I found good girls or boys,
That hated quarrels, strife and noise,

I left an apple, or a tart,
Or wooden gun, or painted cart.

To some I gave a pretty doll,
To some a peg-top, or a ball;
No crackers, cannons, squibs, or rockets,
To blow their eyes up, or their pockets.

No drums to stun their Mother's ear,
Nor swords to make their sisters fear;
But pretty books to store their mind
With knowledge of each various kind.

But where I found the children naughty,
In manners rude, in temper haughty,
Thankless to parents, liars, swearers,
Boxers, or cheats, or base tale-bearers,

I left a long, black, birchen rod,
Such as the dread command of God
Directs a parent's hand to use
When virtue's path his sons refuse.

The Twelve Days of Christmas

ANONYMOUS

The first day of Christmas,
My true love sent to me
A partridge in a pear tree.

The second day of Christmas,
My true love sent to me
Two turtle doves, and
A partridge in a pear tree.

The third day of Christmas,
My true love sent to me
Three French hens,
Two turtle doves, and
A partridge in a pear tree.

The fourth day of Christmas,
My true love sent to me
Four colly birds,
Three French hens,
Two turtle doves, and
A partridge in a pear tree.

The fifth day of Christmas,
My true love sent to me
Five gold rings,
Four colly birds,
Three French hens,
Two turtle doves, and
A partridge in a pear tree.

The sixth day of Christmas,
My true love sent to me
Six geese a-laying,
Five gold rings,
Four colly birds,
Three French hens,
Two turtle doves, and
A partridge in a pear tree.

The seventh day of Christmas,
My true love sent to me
Seven swans a-swimming,
Six geese a-laying,
Five gold rings,
Four colly birds,
Three French hens,
Two turtle doves, and
A partridge in a pear tree.

The eighth day of Christmas,
My true love sent to me
Eight maids a-milking,
Seven swans a-swimming,
Six geese a-laying,
Five gold rings,
Four colly birds,
Three French hens,
Two turtle doves, and
A partridge in a pear tree.

The ninth day of Christmas,
My true love sent to me
Nine drummers drumming,
Eight maids a-milking,
Seven swans a-swimming,
Six geese a-laying,
Five gold rings,
Four colly birds,
Three French hens,
Two turtle doves, and
A partridge in a pear tree.

The tenth day of Christmas,
My true love sent to me
Ten pipers piping,
Nine drummers drumming,
Eight maids a-milking,
Seven swans a-swimming,
Six geese a-laying,
Five gold rings,
Four colly birds,
Three French hens,
Two turtle doves, and
A partridge in a pear tree.

The eleventh day of Christmas
My true love sent to me
Eleven ladies dancing,
Ten pipers piping,
Nine drummers drumming,
Eight maids a-milking,
Seven swans a-swimming,
Six geese a-laying,
Five gold rings,

Four colly birds,
Three French hens,
Two turtle doves, and
A partridge in a pear tree.

The twelfth day of Christmas
My true love sent to me
Twelve fiddlers fiddling,
Eleven ladies dancing,
Ten pipers piping,
Nine drummers drumming,
Eight maids a-milking,
Seven swans a-swimming,
Six geese a-laying,
Five gold rings,
Four colly birds,
Three French hens,
Two turtle doves, and
A partridge in a pear tree.

Ring Out, Wild Bells

ALFRED, LORD TENNYSON

Ring out, wild bells, to the wild sky,
　The flying cloud, the frosty light:
　The year is dying in the night;
Ring out, wild bells, and let him die.

Ring out the old, ring in the new,
　Ring, happy bells, across the snow:
　The year is going, let him go;
Ring out the false, ring in the true.

Ring out the grief that saps the mind
　For those that here we see no more;
　Ring out the feud of rich and poor,
Ring in redress to all mankind.

Ring out a slowly dying cause,
　And ancient forms of party strife;

Ring in the nobler modes of life,
With sweeter manners, purer laws.

Ring out the want, the care, the sin,
  The faithless coldness of the times;
  Ring out, ring out my mournful rhymes
But ring the fuller minstrel in.

Ring out false pride in place and blood,
  The civic slander and the spite;
  Ring in the love of truth and right,
Ring in the common love of good.

Ring out old shapes of foul disease;
  Ring out the narrowing lust of gold;
  Ring out the thousand wars of old,
Ring in the thousand years of peace.

Ring in the valiant man and free,
  The larger heart, the kindlier hand;
  Ring out the darkness of the land,
Ring in the Christ that is to be.

Lordings, Listen to Our Lay

ANONYMOUS

Lordings, listen to our lay—
We have come from far away
    To seek Christmas;
In this mansion we are told
He His yearly feast doth hold:
    'Tis to-day! May joy come from
God above,
To all those who Christmas love.

Jest 'Fore Christmas

EUGENE FIELD

Father calls me William, sister calls me Will,

Mother calls me Willie, but the fellers call me
Bill!

Mighty glad I ain't a girl—ruther be a boy,

Without them sashes, curls, an' things that's
worn by Fauntleroy!

Love to chawnk green apples an' go swimmin' in
the lake—

Hate to take the castor-ile they give for
bellyache!

Most all the time, the whole year round, there
ain't no flies on me,

But jest 'fore Christmas I'm as good as I kin be!

Got a yeller dog named Sport, sick him on the
cat;

First thing she knows she doesn't know where
she is at!

Got a clipper sled, an' when us kids goes out to
    slide,
Long comes the grocery cart, an' we all hook a
    ride!
But sometimes when the grocery man is
    worrited an' cross,
He reaches at us with his whip, an' larrups up
    his hoss,
An' then I laff an' holler, "Oh, ye never teched me!"
But jest 'fore Christmas I'm as good as I kin be!

Gran'ma says she hopes that when I git to be a
    man,
I'll be a missionarer like her oldest brother, Dan,
As was et up by the cannibuls that lives in
    Ceylon's Isle,
Where every prospeck pleases, an' only man is
    vile!
But gran'ma she has never been to see a Wild
    West show,
Nor read the Life of Daniel Boone, or else I
    guess she'd know

That Buff'lo Bill an' cowboys is good enough for
    me!
Excep' jest 'fore Christmas, when I'm good as I
    kin be!

And then old Sport he hangs around, so
    solemn-like an' still,
His eyes they seem a-sayin': "What's the matter,
    little Bill?"
The old cat sneaks down off her perch an'
    wonders what's become
Of them two enemies of hern that used to make
    things hum!
But I am so perlite an' 'tend so earnestly to biz,
That mother says to father: "How improved our
    Willie is!"
But father, havin' been a boy hisself, suspicions
    me
When, jest 'fore Christmas, I'm as good as I kin be!

For Christmas, with its lots an' lots of candies,
    cakes, an' toys,

Was made, they say, for proper kids an' not for
    naughty boys;
So wash yer face an' bresh yer hair, an' mind yer
    p's and q's,
An' don't bust out yer pantaloons, and don't
    wear out yer shoes;
Say "Yessum" to the ladies, an' "Yessur" to the
    men,
An' when they's company, don't pass yer plate
    for pie again;
But, thinkin' of the things yer'd like to see upon
    that tree,
Jest 'fore Christmas be as good as yer kin be!

Spellbound

EMILY BRONTË

The night is darkening round me,
The wild winds coldly blow;
But a tyrant spell has bound me
And I cannot, cannot go.

The giant trees are bending
Their bare boughs weighed with snow.
And the storm is fast descending,
And yet I cannot go.

Clouds beyond clouds above me,
Wastes beyond wastes below;
But nothing drear can move me;
I will not, cannot go.

Christmas at Sea

ROBERT LOUIS STEVENSON

The sheets were frozen hard, and they cut the
    naked hand;
The decks were like a slide, where a seaman
    scarce could stand;
The wind was a nor'wester, blowing squally off
    the sea;
And cliffs and spouting breakers were the only
    things a-lee.

They heard the surf a-roaring before the break
    of day;
But 'twas only with the peep of light we saw
    how ill we lay.
We tumbled every hand on deck instanter, with
    a shout,
And we gave her the maintops'l, and stood by to
    go about.

All day we tacked and tacked between the
    South Head and the North;
All day we hauled the frozen sheets, and got no
    further forth;
All day as cold as charity, in bitter pain and
    dread,
For very life and nature we tacked from head to
    head.

We gave the South a wider berth, for there the
    tide-race roared;
But every tack we made we brought the North
    Head close aboard:
So's we saw the cliffs and houses, and the
    breakers running high,
And the coastguard in his garden, with his glass
    against his eye.

The frost was on the village roofs as white as
  ocean foam;
The good red fires were burning bright in every
  'long-shore home;
The windows sparkled clear, and the chimneys
  volleyed out;
And I vow we sniffed the victuals as the vessel
  went about.

The bells upon the church were rung with a
  mighty jovial cheer;
For it's just that I should tell you how (of all
  days in the year)
This day of our adversity was blessed Christmas
  morn,
And the house above the coastguard's was the
  house where I was born.

O well I saw the pleasant room, the pleasant
  faces there,
My mother's silver spectacles, my father's silver
  hair;

And well I saw the firelight, like a flight of
    homely elves,
Go dancing round the china-plates that stand
    upon the shelves.

And well I knew the talk they had, the talk that
    was of me,
Of the shadow on the household and the son
    that went to sea;
And O the wicked fool I seemed, in every kind
    of way,
To be here and hauling frozen ropes on blessed
    Christmas Day.

They lit the high sea-light, and the dark began
    to fall.
"All hands to loose topgallant sails," I heard the
    captain call.
"By the Lord, she'll never stand it," our first
    mate Jackson, cried.
..."It's the one way or the other, Mr. Jackson," he
    replied.

She staggered to her bearings, but the sails were
new and good,
And the ship smelt up to windward just as
though she understood.
As the winter's day was ending, in the entry of
the night,
We cleared the weary headland, and passed
below the light.

And they heaved a mighty breath, every soul on
board but me,
As they saw her nose again pointing handsome
out to sea;
But all that I could think of, in the darkness and
the cold,
Was just that I was leaving home and my folks
were growing old.

Winter-Time

ROBERT LOUIS STEVENSON

Late lies the wintry sun a-bed,
A frosty, fiery sleepy-head;
Blinks but an hour or two; and then,
A blood-red orange, sets again.

Before the stars have left the skies,
At morning in the dark I rise;
And shivering in my nakedness,
By the cold candle, bathe and dress.

Close by the jolly fire I sit
To warm my frozen bones a bit;
Or with a reindeer-sled, explore
The colder countries round the door.

When to go out, my nurse doth wrap
Me in my comforter and cap;
The cold wind burns my face, and blows
Its frosty pepper up my nose.

Black are my steps on silver sod;
Thick blows my frosty breath abroad;
And tree and house, and hill and lake,
Are frosted like a wedding cake.

Woods in Winter

HENRY WADSWORTH LONGFELLOW

When winter winds are piercing chill,
  And through the hawthorn blows the gale,
With solemn feet I tread the hill,
  That overbrows the lonely vale.

O'er the bare upland, and away
  Through the long reach of desert woods,
The embracing sunbeams chastely play,
  And gladden these deep solitudes.

Where, twisted round the barren oak,
  The summer vine in beauty clung,
And summer winds the stillness broke,
  The crystal icicle is hung.

Where, from their frozen urns, mute springs
  Pour out the river's gradual tide,
Shrilly the skater's iron rings,
  And voices fill the woodland side.

Alas! how changed from the fair scene,
  When birds sang out their mellow lay,
And winds were soft, and woods were green,
  And the song ceased not with the day!

But still wild music is abroad,
  Pale, desert woods! within your crowd;
And gathering winds, in hoarse accord,
  Amid the vocal reeds pipe loud.

Chill airs and wintry winds! my ear
  Has grown familiar with your song;
I hear it in the opening year,
  I listen, and it cheers me long.

Snow-flakes

HENRY WADSWORTH LONGFELLOW

Out of the bosom of the Air,
    Out of the cloud-folds of her garments shaken,
Over the woodlands brown and bare,
    Over the harvest-fields forsaken,
        Silent, and soft, and slow
        Descends the snow.

Even as our cloudy fancies take
    Suddenly shape in some divine expression,
Even as the troubled heart doth make
    In the white countenance confession,
        The troubled sky reveals
        The grief it feels.

This is the poem of the air,
    Slowly in silent syllables recorded;
This is the secret of despair,
    Long in its cloudy bosom hoarded,
        Now whispered and revealed
        To wood and field.

The Meeting

HENRY WADSWORTH LONGFELLOW

After so long an absence
At last we meet again:
Does the meeting give us pleasure,
Or does it give us pain?

The tree of life has been shaken,
And but few of us linger now,
Like the Prophet's two or three berries
In the top of the uppermost bough.

We cordially greet each other
In the old, familiar tone;
And we think, though we do not say it,
How old and gray he is grown!

We speak of a Merry Christmas
And many a Happy New Year;
But each in his heart is thinking

Of those that are not here.
We speak of friends and their fortunes,
And of what they did and said,
Till the dead alone seem living,
And the living alone seem dead.
And at last we hardly distinguish
Between the ghosts and the guests;
And a mist and shadow of sadness
Steals over our merriest jests.

A Song of Christmas

KATHARINE TYNAN

The Christmas moon shines clear and bright;
There were poor travellers such a night
Had neither fire nor candle-light.

One plucked them stars out of the sky
To show the road to travel by;
So that the Ass go warily.

She had all Heaven safe in her hold,
Hidden within her mantle's fold—
All Heaven, and It was one hour old.

Her hair under, over Him spread
His spun-gold coverlet and His bed,
Twined with His little golden head.

She sang and rocked Him to-and-fro
Such songs as little babies know,
With Lullaby Sweet, and Lullalo.

He had no need of moons and suns,
Nor the gold-crested bird-legions,
Singing their lauds and orisons.

The Christmas moon shows a cold beam;
He hath His Mother, she hath Him:
Together they sleep, together dream.

Signs of Christmas

EDWIN LEES

When on the barn's thatch'd roof is seen
The moss in tufts of liveliest green;
When Roger to the wood pile goes,
And, as he turns, his fingers blows;
When all around is cold and drear,
Be sure that Christmas-tide is near.

When up the garden walk in vain
We seek for Flora's lovely train;
When the sweet hawthorn bower is bare,
And bleak and cheerless is the air;
When all seems desolate around,
Christmas advances o'er the ground.

When Tom at eve comes home from plough,
And brings the mistletoe's green bough,
With milk-white berries spotted o'er,
And shakes it the sly maids before,

Then hangs the trophy up on high,
Be sure that Christmas-tide is nigh.

When Hal, the woodman, in his clogs,
Bears home the huge unwieldly logs,
That, hissing on the smould'ring fire,
Flame out at last a quiv'ring spire;
When in his hat the holly stands,
Old Christmas musters up his bands.

When cluster'd round the fire at night,
Old William talks of ghost and sprite,
And, as a distant out-house gate
Slams by the wind, they fearful wait,
While some each shadowy nook explore,
Then Christmas pauses at the door.

When Dick comes shiv'ring from the yard,
And says the pond is frozen hard,
While from his hat, all white with snow,
The moisture, trickling, drops below,
While carols sound, the night to cheer,
Then Christmas and his train are here.

Our Joyful Feast

GEORGE WITHER

So, now is come our joyful feast,
  Let every soul be jolly!
Each room with ivy leaves is drest,
  And every post with holly.
Though some churls at our mirth repine,
Round your brows let garlands twine,
Drown sorrow in a cup of wine,
  And let us all be merry!

Now all our neighbours' chimneys smoke,
  And Christmas logs are burning;
Their ovens with baked meats do choke,
  And all their spits are turning.
Without the door let sorrow lie,
And if for cold it hap to die,
We'll bury it in Christmas pie,
  And evermore be merry!

Now Winter Nights Enlarge

THOMAS CAMPION

Now winter nights enlarge
The number of their hours,
And clouds their storms discharge
Upon the airy towers.
Let now the chimneys blaze,
And cups o'erflow with wine;
Let well-tuned words amaze
With harmony divine.
Now yellow waxen lights
Shall wait on honey love,
While youthful revels, masques, and courtly
    sights
Sleep's leaden spells remove.

The time doth well dispense
With lovers' long discourse;
Much speech hath some defence,
Though beauty no remorse.
All do not all things well:
Some, measures comely tread,
Some, knotted riddles tell,
Some, poems smoothly read.
The summer hath his joys,
And winter his delights;
Though love and all his pleasures are but toys,
They shorten tedious nights.

To Mrs K____, On Her Sending Me an English Christmas Plum-Cake at Paris

HELEN MARIA WILLIAMS

What crowding thoughts around me wake,
What marvels in a Christmas-cake!
Ah say, what strange enchantment dwells
Enclosed within its odorous cells?
Is there no small magician bound
Encrusted in its snowy round?
For magic surely lurks in this,
A cake that tells of vanished bliss;
A cake that conjures up to view
The early scenes, when life was new;
When memory knew no sorrows past,
And hope believed in joys that last!—
Mysterious cake, whose folds contain
Life's calendar of bliss and pain;

That speaks of friends for ever fled,
And wakes the tears I love to shed.
Oft shall I breathe her cherished name
From whose fair hand the offering came:
For she recalls the artless smile
Of nymphs that deck my native isle;
Of beauty that we love to trace,
Allied with tender, modest grace;
Of those who, while abroad they roam,
Retain each charm that gladdens home,
And whose dear friendships can impart
A Christmas banquet for the heart!

The Truce of Christmas

G. K. CHESTERTON

Passionate peace is in the sky—
And in the snow in silver sealed
The beasts are perfect in the field,
And men seem men so suddenly—
(But take ten swords and ten times ten
And blow the bugle in praising men;
For we are for all men under the sun,
And they are against us every one;
And misers haggle and madmen clutch,
And there is peril in praising much.
And we have the terrible tongues uncurled
That praise the world to the sons of the world.)

The idle humble hill and wood
Are bowed upon the sacred birth,
And for one little hour the earth
Is lazy with the love of good—
(But ready are you, and ready am I,
If the battle blow and the guns go by;
For we are for all men under the sun,
And they are against us every one;
And the men that hate herd all together,
To pride and gold, and the great white feather
And the thing is graven in star and stone
That the men who love are all alone.)

Hunger is hard and time is tough,
But bless the beggars and kiss the kings,
For hope has broken the heart of things,
And nothing was ever praised enough.
(But bold the shield for a sudden swing
And point the sword when you praise a thing,
For we are for all men under the sun,
And they are against us every one;
And mime and merchant, thane and thrall
Hate us because we love them all;
Only till Christmastide go by
Passionate peace is in the sky.)

A Christmas Song for Three Guilds

G. K. CHESTERTON

TO BE SUNG A LONG TIME AGO—OR HENCE

THE CARPENTERS

St. Joseph to the Carpenters said on a
    Christmas Day:
"The master shall have patience and the prentice
    shall obey;
And your word unto your women shall be
    nowise hard or wild:
For the sake of me, your master, who have
    worshipped Wife and Child.
But softly you shall frame the fence, and softly
    carve the door,
And softly plane the table—as to spread it for
    the poor,
And all your thoughts be soft and white as the
    wood of the white tree.

But if they tear the Charter, let the tocsin speak
    for me!
Let the wooden sign above your shop be
    prouder to be scarred
Than the lion-shield of Lancelot that hung at
    Joyous Garde."

THE SHOEMAKERS

St. Crispin to the shoemakers said on a
    Christmastide:
"Who fashions at another's feet will get no good
    of pride.
They were bleeding on the Mountain, the feet
    that brought good news,
The latchet of whose shoes we were not worthy
    to unloose.
See that your feet offend not, nor lightly lift
    your head,
Tread softly on the sunlit roads the bright dust
    of the dead.
Let your own feet be shod with peace; be lowly
    all your lives.

But if they touch the Charter, ye shall nail it
with your knives.
And the bill-blades of the commons drive in all
as dense array
As once a crash of arrows came, upon St.
Crispin's Day."

THE PAINTERS

St. Luke unto the painters on Christmas Day he
said:
"See that the robes are white you dare to dip in
gold and red;
For only gold the kings can give, and only blood
the saints;
And his high task grows perilous that mixes
them in paints.
Keep you the ancient order; follow the men that
knew
The labyrinth of black and white, the maze of
green and blue;
Paint mighty things, paint paltry things, paint
silly things or sweet.

But if men break the Charter, you may slay
    them in the street.
And if you paint one post for them, then ... but
    you know it well,
You paint a harlot's face to drag all heroes down
    to hell."

ALL TOGETHER

Almighty God to all mankind on Christmas
   Day said He:

"I rent you from the old red hills and, rending,
   made you free.

There was charter, there was challenge; in a
   blast of breath I gave;

You can be all things other; you cannot be a
   slave.

You shall be tired and tolerant of fancies as they
   fade,

But if men doubt the Charter, ye shall call on
   the Crusade—

Trumpet and torch and catapult, cannon and
   bow and blade,

Because it was My challenge to all the things I
   made."

A Child of the Snows

G. K. CHESTERTON

There is heard a hymn when the panes dim
And never before or again,
When the nights are strong with a darkness
   long,
And the dark is alive with rain.

Never we know but in sleet and in snow,
The place where the great fires are,
That the midst of the earth is a raging mirth
And the heart of the earth a star.

And at night we win to the ancient inn
Where the child in the frost is furled,
We follow the feet where all souls meet
At the inn at the end of the world.

The gods lie dead where the leaves lie red,
For the flame of the sun is flown.
The gods lie cold where the leaves lie gold,
And a Child comes forth alone.

The House of Christmas

G. K. CHESTERTON

There fared a mother driven forth
Out of an inn to roam;
In the place where she was homeless
All men are at home.
The crazy stable close at hand,
With shaking timber and shifting sand,
Grew a stronger thing to abide and stand
Than the square stones of Rome.

For men are homesick in their homes,
And strangers under the sun,
And they lay their heads in a foreign land
Whenever the day is done.
Here we have battle and blazing eyes,
And chance and honour and high surprise,
Where the yule tale was begun.
A Child in a foul stable,

Where the beasts feed and foam;
Only where He was homeless
Are you and I at home;
We have hands that fashion and heads that know
But our hearts we lost—how long ago!
In a place no chart nor ship can show
Under the sky's dome.

This world is wild as an old wives' tale,
And strange the plain things are,
The earth is enough and the air is enough
For our wonder and our war;
But our rest is as far as the fire-drake swings
And our peace is put in impossible things
Where clashed and thundered unthinkable wings
Round an incredible star.

To an open house in the evening
Home shall men come,
To an older place than Eden
And a taller town than Rome.
To the end of the way of the wandering star,
To the things that cannot be and that are,
To the place where God was homeless
And all men are at home.

To M. E. D.

G. K. CHESTERTON

Words, for alas my trade is words, a barren
     burst of rhyme,
   Rubbed by a hundred rhymesters, battered a
     thousand times,
Take them, you, that smile on strings, those
     nobler sounds than mine,
   The words that never lie, or brag, or flatter, or
     malign.

I give a hand to my lady, another to my friend,
   To whom you too have given a hand; and so
     before the end
We four may pray, for all the years, whatever
     suns beset,
   The sole two prayers worth praying—to live
     and not forget.

The pale leaf falls in pallor, but the green leaf
    turns to gold;
  We that have found it good to be young shall
    find it good to be old;
Life that bringeth the marriage bell, the cradle
    and the grave,
  Life that is mean to the mean of heart, and
    only brave to the brave.

In the calm of the last white winter, when all the
    past is ours,
  Old tears are frozen as jewels, old storms
    frosted as flowers.
Dear Lady, may we meet again, stand up again,
    we four,
  Beneath the burden of the years, and praise
    the earth once more.

Winter Evening
from "The Task"

WILLIAM COWPER

Now stir the fire, and close the shutters fast,
  Let fall the curtains, wheel the sofa round,
  And while the bubbling and loud-hissing urn
  Throws up a steamy column, and the cups,
  That cheer but not inebriate, wait on each,
  So let us welcome peaceful evening in.

Oh Winter, ruler of the inverted year,
  Thy scattered hair with sleet-like ashes filled,
  Thy breath congealed upon thy lips, thy
    cheeks
  Fringed with a beard made white with other
    snows
  Than those of age, thy forehead wrapped in
    clouds,
  A leafless branch thy sceptre, and thy throne

A sliding car indebted to no wheels,
But urged by storms along its slippery way,
I love thee, all unlovely as thou seem'st,
And dreaded as thou art. Thou hold'st the sun
A prisoner in the yet undawning East,
Shortening his journey between morn and noon,
And hurrying him, impatient of his stay,
Down to the rosy west; but kindly still
Compensating his loss with added hours
Of social converse and instructive ease,
And gathering at short notice in one group
The family dispersed, and fixing thought
Not less dispersed by daylight and its cares.
I crown thee king of intimate delights,
Fire-side enjoyments, home-born happiness,
And all the comforts that the lowly roof
Of undisturbed retirement, and the hours
Of long uninterrupted evening know.

"Blow, Blow, thou winter wind"

WILLIAM SHAKESPEARE

Blow, blow, thou winter wind,
  Thou art not so unkind
    As man's ingratitude;
  Thy tooth is not so keen,
Because thou art not seen,
    Although thy breath be rude.
Heigh-ho! sing, heigh-ho! unto the green holly:
Most friendship is feigning, most loving mere
    folly:
  Then, heigh-ho, the holly!
    This life is most jolly.
  Freeze, freeze, thou bitter sky,
  That dost not bite so nigh
    As benefits forgot:

Though thou the waters warp,
   Thy sting is not so sharp
   As friend remembered not.
Heigh-ho! sing, heigh-ho! unto the green holly...

Before the Ice is in the Pools

EMILY DICKINSON

Before the ice is in the pools—
Before the skaters go,
Or any check at nightfall
Is tarnished by the snow—

Before the fields have finished,
Before the Christmas tree,
Wonder upon wonder
Will arrive to me!

What we touch the hems of
On a summer's day—
What is only walking
Just a bridge away—

That which sings so—speaks so—
When there's no one here—
Will the frock I wept in
Answer me to wear?

In Drear Nighted December

JOHN KEATS

In drear nighted December,
　Too happy, happy tree,
Thy branches ne'er remember
　Their green felicity—
The north cannot undo them
With a sleety whistle through them
Nor frozen thawings glue them
　From budding at the prime.

In drear-nighted December,
　Too happy, happy brook,
Thy bubblings ne'er remember
　Apollo's summer look;
But with a sweet forgetting,
They stay their crystal fretting,

Never, never petting
   About the frozen time.

Ah! would 'twere so with many
   A gentle girl and boy—
But were there ever any
   Writh'd not of passed joy?
The feel of not to feel it,
When there is none to heal it
Nor numbed sense to steel it,
   Was never said in rhyme.

To a Locomotive in Winter

WALT WHITMAN

Thee for my recitative,
Thee in the driving storm even as now, the snow,
    the winter-day declining,
Thee in thy panoply, thy measur'd dual
    throbbing and thy beat convulsive,
Thy black cylindric body, golden brass, and
    silvery steel,
Thy ponderous side-bars, parallel and
    connecting rods, gyrating, shuttling at thy
    sides,
Thy metrical, now swelling pant and roar, now
    tapering in the distance,
Thy great protruding head-light fix'd in front,
Thy long, pale, floating vapor-pennants, tinged
    with delicate purple,

The dense and murky clouds out-belching from
    thy smoke-stack,
Thy knitted frame, thy springs and valves, the
    tremulous twinkle of thy wheels,
Thy train of cars behind, obedient, merrily
    following,
Through gale or calm, now swift, now slack, yet
    steadily careering;
Type of the modern—emblem of motion and
    power—pulse of the continent,
For once come serve the Muse and merge in
    verse, even as here I see thee,
With storm and buffeting gusts of wind and
    falling snow,
By day thy warning ringing bell to sound its
    notes,
By night thy silent signal lamps to swing.

Fierce-throated beauty!

Roll through my chant with all thy lawless
music, thy swinging lamps at night,

Thy madly-whistled laughter, echoing, rumbling
like an earthquake, rousing all,

Law of thyself complete, thine own track firmly
holding,

(No sweetness debonair of tearful harp or glib
piano thine,)

Thy trills of shrieks by rocks and hills
return'd,

Launch'd o'er the prairies wide, across the
lakes,

To the free skies unpent and glad and strong.

London Snow

ROBERT BRIDGES

When men were all asleep the snow came flying,
In large white flakes falling on the city brown,
Stealthily and perpetually settling and loosely
   lying,
   Hushing the latest traffic of the drowsy town;
Deadening, muffling, stifling its murmurs failing;
Lazily and incessantly floating down and down:
   Silently sifting and veiling road, roof and
   railing;
Hiding difference, making unevenness even,
Into angles and crevices softly drifting and sailing.
   All night it fell, and when full inches seven
It lay in the depth of its uncompacted lightness,
The clouds blew off from a high and frosty heaven;
   And all woke earlier for the unaccustomed
   brightness
Of the winter dawning, the strange unheavenly
   glare:

The eye marvelled—marvelled at the dazzling
    whiteness;
    The ear hearkened to the stillness of the
    solemn air;
No sound of wheel rumbling nor of foot falling,
And the busy morning cries came thin and
    spare.
    Then boys I heard, as they went to school,
    calling,
They gathered up the crystal manna to freeze
Their tongues with tasting, their hands with
    snowballing;
    Or rioted in a drift, plunging up to the
    knees;
Or peering up from under the white-mossed
    wonder,
'O look at the trees!' they cried, 'O look at the
    trees!'
    With lessened load a few carts creak and
    blunder,
Following along the white deserted way,
A country company long dispersed asunder:

When now already the sun, in pale display
Standing by Paul's high dome, spread forth
    below
His sparkling beams, and awoke the stir of the
    day.
    For now doors open, and war is waged with
    the snow;
And trains of sombre men, past tale of number,
Tread long brown paths, as toward their toil
    they go:
    But even for them awhile no cares encumber
Their minds diverted; the daily word is
    unspoken,
The daily thoughts of labour and sorrow
    slumber
At the sight of the beauty that greets them, for
    the charm they have broken.